BURFORD
IN OLD PHOTOGRAPHS

BURFORD
IN OLD PHOTOGRAPHS

COLLECTED BY
ALFRED JEWELL

ALAN SUTTON
1985

Alan Sutton Publishing Limited
Brunswick Road · Gloucester

First published 1985

British Library Cataloguing in Publication Data

Burford in old photographs.
1. Burford (Oxfordshire)—History
I. Jewell, Alfred
942.5'71   DA690.B92

ISBN 0-86299-224-9

Typesetting and origination by
Alan Sutton Publishing Limited.
Printed in Great Britain.

CONTENTS

INTRODUCTION

Originally a Saxon settlement situated on the edge of the Cotswolds, Burford has developed gradually over the years into a prosperous small town. Much of its early prosperity was due to the wool trade in the area. Now, with its many fine buildings of local stone, and the beautiful church with its majestic spire standing by the River Windrush, it is one of the most picturesque small towns in the Cotswolds and attracts a huge number of visitors throughout the year.

The following collection of photographs takes a look back in time to show some scenes of Burford as it was in the past. They date from the late 1800s to the middle of the 1900s. Although a great number of changes have taken place in the town during the past years, it is interesting to notice that many of the buildings have changed very little in outward appearance. There were various shops to cater for most requirements, and bread was delivered by the baker with his donkey and cart from his shop in Sheep Street. The town had its own brewery, but beer has not been brewed on the premises since 1969.

Among the many skilled craftsmen in Burford were saddlers, tinsmiths, and the blacksmith who was often seen shoeing a horse on the pavement outside the forge. The town also had a bell foundry in Witney Street.

Gone are the days when the clatter of hooves announced the arrival of the coach and four on their way from Gloucester to London – a number of coaches passed through Burford from larger towns. Later, came the age of the railways, when horsedrawn buses took passengers to the stations at Shipton and Witney. They were run by Mr Paintin who also owned the Temperance Hotel in Sheep Street where weary travellers could rest.

Street fairs were popular in the town, and twice a year the Hiring Fair was held in Sheep Street. Here a farmer would offer a shilling to a workman, such as a shepherd or carter, and if the shilling was accepted the man was hired for six months. Pageants were great occasions in the early 1900s, and the meet of the Heythrop Hunt always attracted many onlookers. The town had its own agricultural show, which was often held at Chapmans Piece, a paddock in Witney Street.

The adjoining village of Fulbrook is across the River Windrush on the north side of the town. It is a charming little Cotswold village and the residents always helped and joined in with Burford to arrange pageants and other social events.

I have been collecting old photographs of Burford and Fulbrook for several years, and it has been very enjoyable. I am very grateful to everyone who has helped, especially those who have kindly loaned their photographs for copying, thereby making it possible to produce this book. I hope this glimpse of the past will interest all those who know this lovely town.

THE TOLSEY, 1863, showing a sun dial facing east. The house above has a slate roof with dormer windows.

THE TOLSEY, 1890, now has a clock. The house above has been altered to a three storey building in Victorian style.

HIGH STREET, 1870. The George Inn is on the left.

THE BURFORD BUS, outside the Bull Hotel, 1888.

Paintin & Son's Omnibuses,

(THE ORIGINAL PROMOTERS.)

Run to Shipton three times daily, meeting the 8.2, 8.41 and 12 a.m. ; 12.36, 4.25, and 4.47 p.m. Trains.

Starting at 7-5, 10-50 and 3-15.

For Witney at 11 daily, for 12.25 train for Oxford and London

waiting for the 5 Train at Witney.

FARE 1/- EACH WAY.

Passengers called for or fetched in from any distance..

CONTRACTORS H.M. MAILS.

The Cheapest House in the Town for Excursion or Pleasure Parties.

Horses and Broughams, Cabs, Dog Carts, Wagonettes, Omnibuses.

Wedding Carriages on the shortest notice.

BATH CHAIR, with Rubber Tyres, for Hire.

Funeral Car kept on the Premises.

'Lenthall' Temperance Hotel.

Every Accommodation at Moderate Charges.

Letters and Telegrams receive prompt attention.

Telegraphic Address: Paintins, Burford.

PAINTINS' OMNIBUS TIMETABLE, 1880s.

A GABLE HOUSE, 1880s. Now a butcher's shop.

WYATTS HARNESS SHOP, 1900s.

CLUB DAY, 1900s. People would invest a few pence into a slate club; if sick they could draw some money every week, otherwise the money was paid out to them at Christmas.

HIGH STREET, 1870s, without trees up the hill.

HIGH STREET, 1888.

HIGH STREET, 1901. The man on the right appears to be painting the lamp post.

WYSDOM COTTAGE, Lower High Street, 1890s. Now the Surgery.

GEORGE YARD, HIGH STREET, 1895. This was a part of the Old George Inn.

STREET FAIR, 1900s.

THE HILL, 1900s.

HIGH STREET, 1901.

HIGH STREET, 1900s.

THE PRIORY, before renovation, 1900s. An Anglican order of nuns now reside in the priory.

GUILDENFORD, early 1900.

RETURN OF THE QUAKERS, 1890s. Tiverton Villa, Guildenford.

SHEEP STREET, 1890s, showing a collection of beer barrels outside the Brewery.

SHEEP STREET, 1890s. Baker-boy.

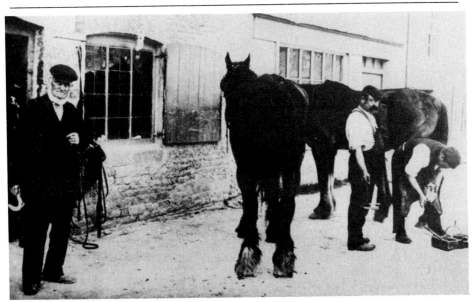

THE SMITHY, 1890s. Hall and Sons.

THE SMITHY, 1890s. Young Bill Hall.

SHEEP STREET, 1890s. Mr Titcomb the baker, with his handcart.

HIGH STREET, early 1900s. Mr Titcomb the baker, with donkey and cart.

CHARLES EAST, 1890s. Engineer working on water wheels.

THE HILL, 1890s, showing gas lamp and a water bucket.

THE ALMSHOUSES, CHURCH GREEN, 1890s.

LENTHALL TEMPERANCE HOTEL, SHEEP STREET, 1890s. This building is now The Countryman offices. Above and top right: Mr Paintin, cab drivers and staff. Bottom right: Paintins' coach and brewer's dray.

SHEEP STREET, 1906. Horse-riders outside the Temperance Hotel.

SHEEP STREET, 1905.

SHEEP STREET, 1908, showing the porch on the Baytree Hotel.

HIGH STREET, 1909.

OLD COLLEGIANS. The tenants standing outside a row of cottages called College Yard, just off the High Street.

Olden Times, Burford Hiring Fair.   N° 52

Sheep St Burford Fair Day.

SHEEP STREET, early 1900s. The Hiring Fair (taking the shilling).

The Lamb Hotel, Sheep Street

High Street

DECORATIONS FOR THE CORONATION OF EDWARD VII, 1902.

Glenthorne House, The Hill

DECORATIONS FOR THE CORONATION OF EDWARD VII, 1902.

The Bull Hotel, High Street

The Grammar School

DECORATIONS FOR THE CORONATION OF EDWARD VII, 1902.

THE HILL, 1906.

SHEEP STREET, 1906. Wyatt's coaches outside the Lamb Hotel. These would take passengers from Burford to Bampton Station.

SHEEP STREET, 1907. Outside the Temperance Hotel.

PRIORY LANE, 1904.

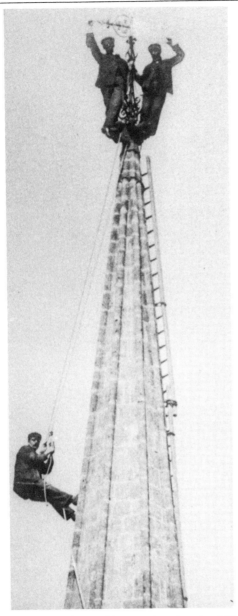

CHURCH STEEPLE, 1907. Steeplejacks working on the church of St John the Baptist.

HIGH STREET, 1910. Forests Boot and Shoe Stores later moved its stock to another premises in High Street and took the name of Bristol House with them.

HIGH STREET, 1907.

HIGH STREET. Three local gentlemen sitting outside Bowermans Antique Shop. Left to right:
Mr Richards, Mr Bowerman, Mr Paintin.

PRIORY LANE, 1908. Spring Fair, 7th April — snow-covered.

COTSWOLD GATEWAY HOTEL. Outside is the sign 'BURFORD — the grey old town on the lonely down'.

ELIZABETHAN PAGENT. 1908.

ELIZABETHAN PAGEANT, 1908.

ARGYLLS MARCHING UP HIGH STREET, 1909.

YEOMEN MARCHING UP HIGH STREET, 1909.

HIGH STREET, 1910. Post office and postmen.

HIGH STREET, 1910. Bowermans antique shop; this is now a restaurant.

HIGH STREET, 1910.

THE HILL, 1910.

CHURCH GREEN, 1920s.

THE MASONS ARMS WITNEY STREET, 1911. (Thirsty work.)

HIGH STREET, 1909. A group of children outside T. Blackwell, basket maker. This is now a ladies' fashion shop.

THE HILL, date unknown. The banner reads 'East Cotswold Art Exhibition'.

THE HILL, 1915. The Swan Inn later became a flower and gift shop for many years, and is now an antique shop.

HIGH STREET, 1915. Note the canopy over the window of the Grammar School gymnasium on the left.

PRIORY LANE CORNER, 1910. The fair leaving town.

THE FAIR, 1920s. Rowels of Burford Steam Roundabouts.

THE FAIR, PRIORY LANE, 1920. An Edward Forest Roundabout.

THE FAIR, 1920s. Caravans parked in the High Street.

WYCHWOOD TOY COMPANY, 1915. Stall selling locally-made toys.

THE HILL, 1918.

CHURCH GREEN, 1917. Home Guards.

THE WESLEYAN CHAPEL IN THE HIGH STREET, 1910.

THE CHURCH, 1920s. Photographed from the meadow which is now the car park.

SCHOOL BUILDING, 1910. This was at the rear of the church house and has now been demolished.

THE RECTORY, PRIORY LANE, 1920s.

THE OLD MILL HOUSE, 1920s. Now called Island House.

LOWER HIGH STREET, 1924. Opening of the girls' grammar school by Mr Horniman, third from the left in the trilby hat.

LOWER HIGH STREET, 1924. Opening of the girls' grammar school.

HIGH STREET, 1920s. E.F. Aldridge, cycle maker, outside The Three Pigeons, now The Mermaid.

HIGH STREET, 1930s. E.F. Aldridge, outside his shop. This is now called London House and is an antique shop.

THE HEYTHROP HUNT, 1934. The meet leaving the town.

WATCHING THE MEET. Above: The Tolsey, 1923. Below: outside the chemist's shop, 1930.

WATCHING THE MEET. Above: the east side of the High Street, 1930. Below: the same spot in 1931.

WATCHING THE MEET. Above: the east side of the High Street, 1934. Below: the west side of the High Street, 1934.

R.A.O.B. WYCHWOOD LODGE CHURCH PARADE, 26 June 1926.

R.A.O.B. WYCHWOOD LODGE CHURCH PARADE, 26 June 1926.

WITNEY STREET, 1926. Tom Bond's Bell Foundry.

WITNEY STREET. Tom Bond working in the Bell Foundry.

WITNEY STREET, 1920s. Mr Chapman standing in the doorway of his cottage.

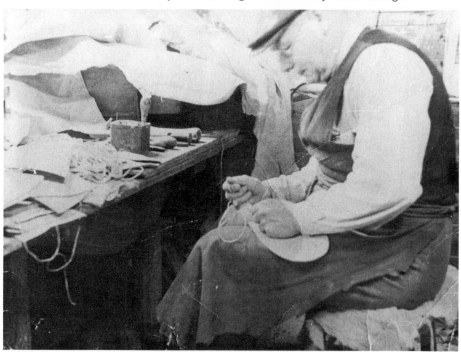

TAN YARD, WITNEY STREET, 1924. Albert Hudson working very skilfully on a pair of leather gloves.

WITNEY STREET, 1920s, showing Bowl's harness-maker's shop.

WITNEY STREET. Mr W. Bowl stitching a saddle: a very skilled craftsman.

HIGH STREET, 1924.

HIGH STREET, 1920s.

WITNEY STREET, 1920s. The Great House, the home of Lord and Lady Piercy for many years.

BURFORD AND FULBROOK W.I. FLOWER SHOW, 3 August 1925.

BURFORD AND FULBROOK W.I. PAGEANT GROUP outside the Falkland Hall, 1 July 1926.

BURFORD AND FULBROOK W.I. PAGEANT GROUP outside the Falkland Hall, 1 July 1926. Note the weighbridge in the foreground.

PRIORY LANE, 1920s, showing a corner of the Falkland Hall.

SHEEP STREET, 1920s. Mrs Titcomb, wife of the baker, who also kept a sweet shop.

PRIORY LANE, 1920s. Mr Smith, the refuse collector.

TANNERS LANE, 1920s. Dennis Rowles, fishmonger.

HIGH STREET, 1920s. A chat with the law.

THE TOLSEY, 1930s. The Mills family waiting for a bus.

BURFORD FOLK DANCERS, 1926. Left to right, back row: M. Wickins, V. Wall, Mrs Kettlewell, F. Wall, D. Honeychurch. Front row: W. Francis, N. Midwinter, M. Francis, H. Barrett.

BURFORD FOLK DANCERS, 1926. Left to right, back row: M. Wickins, V. Wall, F. Wall, M. Francis, D, Honeychurch. Front row: W. Francis, N. Midwinter, H. Barratt.

THE HILL, 1930s, on a quiet day.

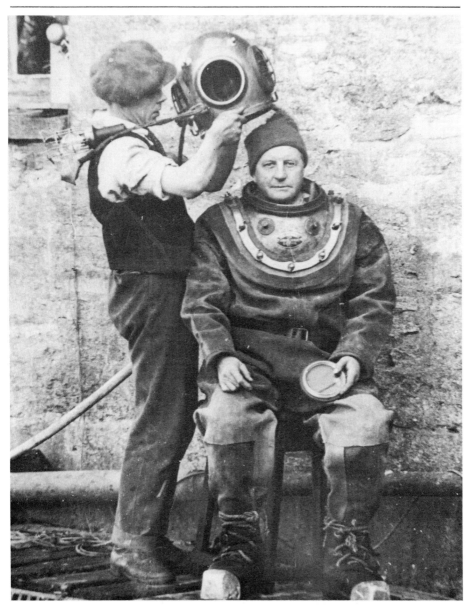

THE BURFORD DIVER, 1927. Three photographs taken at the old mill in Witney street, showing the preparation to inspect the turbine which supplied the town's electricity. Above: the diver, Mr Nolder, almost ready, the helmet being placed on his head by Mr J Brown. Opposite: above, J. Brown, M. Harrod, Mr. Nolder, W. Barrett, M. Bartlett; below, left to right: W. Barrett, M. Harrod, J. Brown, Mr Nolder, M. Bartlett.

THE HILL, 1920s, when parking was no problem.

GUILDENFORD BRIDGE, 1920s. Now demolished and replaced by a new bridge for the car park.

THE HILL, 1926. The Bartlett family walking up the hill by the war memorial.

FIRE BRIGADE BY THE TOLSEY. Date not known. Horse-drawn and manual pump.

N.F.S. (FIRE SERVICE). Left to right, R. Paine, M. Hicks, J. Hicks, N. Barrett, C. Wilkins, G. Hicks, W. Search, B. Hitchcock, A. Francis, W. Dixon.

THE HILL, 1930s. A flock of sheep going down the hill.

WITNEY STREET, 1920s. Mr Holloway's Model T Ford.

THE LAMB HOTEL, SHEEP STREET.

THE HILL, 1920s. Clinch's steam lorry making a delivery of beer to the Bull Hotel.

THE HIGH STREET, 1921.

WITNEY STREET, 1920s.

WITNEY STREET, 1930s.

THE BRIDGE, 1920s. Looking across to Westhall Hill. The elm trees have now gone.

THE CHURCH, 1925. View from a riverside garden.

PRIORY LANE, 1920s. The building with the sign hanging on the wall was the Chip Shop.

BURFORD GOLF CLUB HOUSE, 1929. This building was demolished in 1966 to make way for the roundabout on the main road.

THE BRIDGE, late 1920s. Drawing water for repairs to the A40.

105

LAWRENCE LANE, late 1920s. The sheds on the left were later demolished and replaced by a small house.

THE CHURCH, 1920s. Repairing the lead-work.

GEORGE YARD, 1920s. The cottages have now been converted to homes for senior citizens.

BULL HOTEL YARD, early 1930s, showing a garage at the rear.

THE HILL, 1930s.

HIGH STREET, 1930s.

HIGH STREET, late 1920s.

HIGH STREET, 1930s. Pageant procession through the town.

THE BURFORD ROVERS, 1932.

STURT FARM, near Burford, late 1920s.

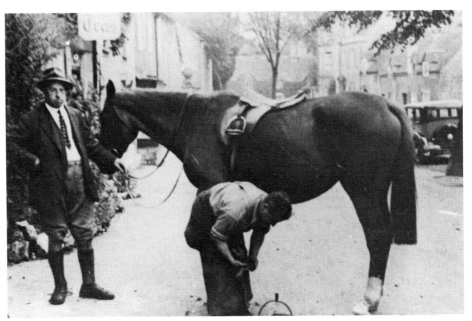

THE BLACKSMITH, Mr B. Hall shoeing Mr Bright's horse outside the forge.

THE BELL RINGERS, 1933. Left to right, back row: B. Hudson, W. Brunsdon, T. Bond. Middle row: H. Barrett, C. Cook, F. Soden. Front row: H. Bond, G. Parker.

GENTLEMEN OF THE JURY, 1937. Seven local businessmen reporting to the court for jury service. The case was the murder of a little girl. Left to right: F. Lomas, J. Wiggins, F.W. Newman, H. Whipp, E. Reavley, A. Weller, E. Aldridge.

WITNEY STREET, 1930s, looking towards High Street.

WITNEY STREET, 1930s.

THE HILL, 1930s.

THE COTSWOLD GATEWAY HOTEL, 1933. Greyhound coach calls at Burford after 80 years.

THE COTSWOLD GATEWAY HOTEL, 1936. AA patrolman, Mr A. Weller.

SHEEP STREET, 1937. Mr O. Burton and Mr F. Wilkinson outside the Brewery.

COTTAGE ON THE CORNER OF SHEEP STREET AND TANNERS LANE, 1933.

LOWER HIGH STREET, 1936, showing the sign for the Bear Inn.

LOWER HIGH STREET, 1938. Many signs for 'Teas'.

THE POST OFFICE, 1938. Now the Priory Tea Rooms.

CANON EMERIS, 1920s. Former Vicar of Burford from 1907–1937.

QUEEN MARY VISITS BURFORD, 1939. Walking towards the church with the Rev. Scott Tucker, Vicar of Burford from 1937–1972.

QUEEN MARY, with Lord and Lady Southby, who lived at the Priory at the time.

THE TOWN BAND, early 1900s. Left to right, back row: B. Hudson, L. Day, W. Aldridge, N. Barrett, F. Smith. Middle row: E. Barrett, E. Mustoe, C. Trinder, G. Haggett, T. Price, G. Houltom, H. Barratt, F. Soden. Front row: A. Timms, G. Hyde, F. Parrott, T. Bond (bandmaster), H. Preston, G. Imms, F. Francis.

THE TOWN BAND, date and names unknown.

SCHOOL GROUP. Outside the Church House, 1890s.

SCHOOL GROUP, early 1900s.

SCHOOL GROUP, 1915.

SCHOOL GROUP, 1920s.

YOUNGEST OF THE BISHOP FAMILY
IRENES AUNTS AND UNCLE
DEFINITELY IDENTIFIED IN THE OTHER
WELFARE BOOK

SCHOOL GROUP, 1920s.

SCHOOL GROUP, 1920s.

SCHOOL GROUP, 1920s.

SCHOOL TEACHERS, late 1920s.

SCHOOL GROUP, late 1920s.

SCHOOL COOKERY CLASS, 1935.

BURFORD TOWN FOOTBALL CLUB, 1898–9. Left to right, back row: A. Jones, G. Hambidge, C. Jeffs, Rowland, C. Evans, ? , Preston, B. Holtom. Front row: Paintin, Walker, H. Millen, R. Newman, E. Hunt, G. Pratley, Wiseman, E. Aldridge.

BURFORD TOWN FOOTBALL CLUB, 1929. Left to right, back row: W. Pratley, F. Timms, H. Kearse, Cpt. Kettlewell, A. Cook, G. Vickers, Griffiths, A. Goodin. Middle row: J. Adams, W. Josey, R. Beckinsale. Front row: L. Forest, E. Forest, J. Goodin, T. Forest, F. Timms.

BURFORD GRAMMAR SCHOOL FOOTBALL TEAM, 1930–1. Names unknown.

BURFORD GRAMMAR SCHOOL RUGBY TEAM, 1931. Names unknown.

BURFORD GRAMMAR SCHOOL CRICKET TEAM, 1935. Names unknown.

BURFORD COTTGE HOSPITAL, early 1900s.

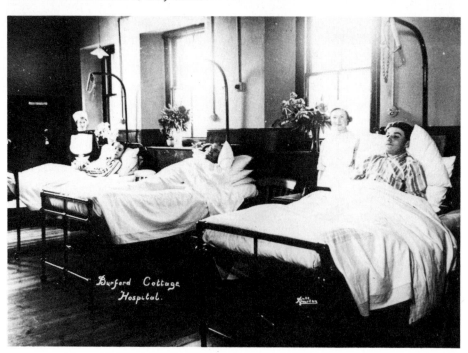

BURFORD COTTAGE HOSPITAL, date unknown.

SHEEP STREET, 1940s. On parade.

THE HOME GUARD, 1940s. Left to right, back row: D. Brown, W. Griffin, T. Townsend, R. Woodward, W. Goodall, B. Winfield, A. Parker, R. Barnard, B. Parker, E. Herbert, M. Stallard, S. Crook, R. Warner, H. Crook, B. Pitts. Front row: A. Herbert, R. Garne, E. Lambert, J. Brown, M. Cook, T. Midwinter, J. Smith, F. Hambidge, J. Coleman.

THE BRIDGE, 1943. A Sherman tank with a broken track crashed through the parapet wall.

COTTAGES OPPOSITE THE COTSWOLD GATEWAY HOTEL. These were demolished in 1966 to make way for the roundabout on the main road.

FULBROOK

MANOR FARM HOUSE, WESTHALL HILL, 1915.

NORMAN CHURCH OF ST JAMES, 1920s.

SCHOOL CHILDREN, early 1900s, after attending church service.

MASONS ARMS PUBLIC HOUSE AND GROCER'S SHOP, 1930s.

CARPENTERS ARMS PUBLIC HOUSE, 1930s.

CORNER COTTAGE, 1890s. Now converted into a studio.

SHIPTON ROAD, 1912. Note the drinking trough in the stream.

CATTLE YARD WITH THATCH ROOF, 1909.

MANOEUVRES, WESTHALL HILL TRIANGLE, 1909.

GUN CARRIAGE AT ELM FARM, 1909.

THE WAR MEMORIAL, 1920s, with the Harris children sitting on the green. The house on the left is called The Limes.

SHIPTON ROAD, 1930s. Mr A. Pratley with a horse and cart.

A GROUP OF WORKMEN, 1927. The men made a cut through the River Windrush.

SCHOOL GROUP, 1901.

SCHOOL GROUP, 1920s

SCHOOL GROUP, 1920s.

SCHOOL GROUP, late 1920s.

LOCAL INHABITANTS, 1920s. Left to right: L. Wilks, A. Forest, L. Forest, F. Smith, E. Wilks, J. Gough, E. Dixon, J. Spinner, E. Wilks. Sitting: W. Dixon, F. Bayliss.

CORONATION FESTIVITY, 1937.

A FULBROOK WEDDING GROUP, 1900s.

PHOTOGRAPH CREDITS

Mrs S. Adams • Miss D. Aldridge • B. Arnold • W.H. Bartlett • G. Batts
R. Bowerman • B. Brown • Mrs N. Brown • P. Caine • Miss D. Chapman
Mrs A. Cook • Mrs C. Cook • Miss D. Cook • H. Crook • J. Dixon • A. Edwards
Mrs C. Forest B. Francis • Miss A. Gough • Miss E. Gough • M. Hall
Mrs. G. Hickman • R.G. Hicks • Mrs I. Holloway • Mrs S.M. Jewell • F. Lomas
Mrs J. Moody • Miss D. Neville • F.W. Newman • F. Packer • Miss L. Paintin
R. Pearman • T. Pether • Mrs E. Pratley • Mrs L. Pratley • C. Roberts
Miss B. Smith • Mrs V. Storie • Mrs J. Swanson • G. Swinford • M. Taubenheim
A. Timms • Mrs A. Vickers • Mrs M. Walker • Mr F. Wilkinson • Mrs M. Wilks
P. Wise